Hope
For Your Children
Even When Things Don't Look So Good

By: Angie Buhrke

Testimony By: Kristin Buhrke Assis

Hope For Your Children: Even When Things Don't Look So Good

© 2016 Angie Buhrke

ISBN 13 TP: 978-0-692-69105-2

Unless otherwise identified, Scripture quotations are taken from the King James Version of the Bible. (Public Domain) Scripture quotations marked (AMPCE) are taken from the Amplified Bible, Copyright © 1954, 1958, 1962, 1964, 1965, 1987 by The Lockman Foundation. Used by permission.

All rights reserved-This book is protected by the copyright laws of the United States of America. No part of this publication may be reproduced or transmitted in any form or by any means without written permission from the publisher.

Editor: Rose Rust

Book & Cover design: Nikki Hitchcock

Printed in the United States of America

Table of Contents

Acknowledgements..5
Introduction...7
Chapter 1: *They Belong to God*..........................21
Chapter 2: *Get Rid of Worry*..............................27
Chapter 3: *A Simple First Step*..........................35
Chapter 4: *Cast Your Care*.................................45
Chapter 5: *Think Right!*......................................53
Chapter 6: *Speak Right!*......................................63
Chapter 7: *Pray Right!*...71
Chapter 8: *Take Your Authority!*........................79
Chapter 9: *Be Careful What You Hear*...............91
Chapter 10: *Forgive*..99
Chapter 11: *Giving*..109
Chapter 12: *Don't Give Up!*...............................117
Chapter 13: *Kristin's Story*.................................125
Final Thoughts..135
Prayer For Your Children.....................................139
Prayer For You..143
Suggested Readings..149

With Gratitude...

I want to thank my Lord and my Savior, Jesus Christ, for His faithfulness to our family during the difficult times expressed in this book. I am grateful to Him for giving me this opportunity to share with other parents what He has taught me that has brought total restoration and victory to our family. Thank You, Jesus.

A special thank you to my husband, Al, who encouraged me to write this book and who demonstrates, more than anyone else I know, the unconditional love of God not only to others, but also to me, personally. Love you, honey.

I want to thank my daughter, Kristin, for her humility in being willing to share her struggles as a teenager and how God has turned it all around. I'm proud of you, Kristin.

And a big thank you to Andrew Wommack for sharing his life-changing revelation with us. Thank you, Andrew!

Introduction

Now the God of hope fill you with all joy and peace in believing, that ye may abound in hope, through the power of the Holy Ghost.

Romans 15:13

"My children are taught of the Lord and great is their peace." (Isaiah 54:13) I repeated this Scripture out loud over and over again one day as I left my daughter's home in tears. But from what I could see, no one was getting through to her, not even God.

I am excited about writing this book for several reasons. My husband and I raised three children and have learned much over the years, both through our mistakes and accomplishments. I believe that you, the parent, will be helped and encouraged while facing some of the same challenges you may have with your children as we did.

Hope For Your Children

One complaint I hear from parents is that they did everything right; they raised their children in a Christian home and taught them Biblical principles of morality and responsibility. Yet, it seemed like in just one day, they turned their back on all they were taught by pursuing their own ungodly desires.

Parents, I know you want answers. You want to know how your child could be happy and carefree in his or her early years, only to become a depressed and miserable young adult. You want to know how your child could receive an award for never missing Sunday School, only to become an alcoholic as a teen. You want to know how your child could be valedictorian in college, only to become addicted to illegal drugs soon after.

After raising our daughter in a Godly home, I wondered for years why she decided to rebel and become pregnant at age 18. It seemed to me that we were experiencing the same problems as non-believers were.

All the above concerns are valid, and although we know some of the reasons why these things

Introduction

happen, the most important thing to know is how to stand for your children in the midst of their struggles.

Recently, I was visiting my 84 year-old dad. As he was watching the evening news, he looked sad. When I asked him what was wrong, he began telling me the way life used to be and how we have lost sight of the important things. Seeing the culture head downhill was hard for him to bear.

He was right. Our culture was once moral and decent. Today it is evil.

This know also, that in the last days perilous times shall come. For men shall be lovers of their own selves, covetous, boasters, proud, blasphemers, disobedient to parents, unthankful, unholy, Without natural affection, trucebreakers, false accusers, incontinent, fierce, despisers of those that are good, Traitors, heady, highminded, lovers of pleasures more than lovers of God; Having a form of godliness, but denying the power thereof: from such turn away. (2 Tim 3:1-5)

The word *perilous* simply means "difficult." We

are definitely seeing difficult times today.

Before I share some reasons why I believe our children may be going astray, I want to make sure you understand that God is not one of those reasons. Many Christians believe that God brings problems into their lives to either teach them something or to punish them for something they have done. I've heard parents say that when they were young their own parents used to tell them, "May your children do to you what you are doing to me." You may recall hearing something like that which may lead you to think that your problems with your children are payback for what you have done.

God does not bring problems; He is the author of good only. He does not bring evil to anyone; it's not in His nature because His nature is Love. It's ridiculous to think that our omnipresent (being present everywhere), omnipotent (having unlimited power), and omniscient (infinitely wise) Heavenly Father could not come up with another way to teach us His principles, other than bringing terrible trials into our lives. Here is how God corrects us...

Introduction

by His Word:

All scripture is given by inspiration of God, and is profitable for doctrine, for reproof, for correction, for instruction in righteousness: That the man of God may be perfect, thoroughly furnished unto all good works. (2 Tim. 3:16-17)

Sometimes we learn through our trials and that's good, but our problems do not come from our loving God.

Here are some of the reasons our children struggle: Our present day media plays a big part. Filth and violence are pumped out all over the internet, television screens, movie theaters, video games and music. The devil is using whoever is willing (it's a choice whom we serve) to be his instruments in bringing evil to the forefront of our society causing demonic activity.

An example would be today's rock music. Most parents are not aware that many song artists worship the devil. A very popular female singer publicly stated that she sold her soul to the devil. Her parents are pastors of a church and it was a very sad day when her dad had to publicly speak out against his own daughter. He said he was more saddened that she was leading millions of young people astray with her music.

There was a rock group in the 1970's who also pledged allegiance to the devil. One of its musicians said, "We can't curse the Christians, but we can get them to curse themselves through our music." How? As they listen to the words, which were prayed over by satanists, demonic activity begins in their mind.

We kill unborn babies; men marry men and women marry women, and if we aren't happy being a man, then we become a woman or vice-versa. These are just some of the things our children are up against. My husband once said that it really isn't fair that we, as parents, now have to fight against the culture to save our kids. It shouldn't be this way.

Another reason why I believe our children are having problems is because of the devil, himself. He attacks Christians simply because they are a threat to

Introduction

him. If he sees Christian parents who are serving the Lord, or in ministry reaching others for Jesus, and knows that they are fully committed to God, then he tries to attack their children to get them off track.

We are protective of our children, especially when they are young, and the devil knows it. So he figures the only way he can shake our faith is to lure our kids and then maybe that would be what it takes to get us to reject God or at least question Him. If he can't get to us, he will try to mess with our children's minds to lead them astray. This works because our children are not yet grounded in the Word, leaving them open to all sorts of assault in their thought life.

So now we can understand why we may have some of the same problems as non-believers. But the good news is that God showed me that if we stand in faith, these problems will pass much more quickly than for those who do not trust God. When He redeems the situation, there will be a testimony that could save the lives of thousands of others that unbelievers may not have.

But the causes of your situation are not what really matters. Look at John 9:2-7:

And his disciples asked him, saying, Master, who did sin, this man, or his parents, that he was born blind? Jesus answered, Neither hath this man sinned, nor his parents: but that the works of God should be made manifest in him. I must work the works of him that sent me, while it is day: the night cometh, when no man can work. As long as I am in the world, I am the light of the world. When he had thus spoken, he spat on the ground, and made clay of the spittle, and he anointed the eyes of the blind man with the clay, And said unto him, Go, wash in the pool of Siloam, (which is by interpretation, Sent). He went his way therefore, and washed, and came seeing.

Reading this passage indicates that Jesus is not really interested in what caused the blindness. Although we can learn from the "why," we need not focus on it because Jesus didn't focus on why this man was born blind. It may or may not have been

Introduction

sin. Jesus was only interested in what could be done about it. He was only interested in bringing glory to His Father by healing this man.

Let me personalize this. You may be thinking that your children acted in a certain way because of the movies they've been watching. That may be true, and it would be good advice to let them know that they are feeding themselves with ungodly principles and hopefully they would refrain from watching what could hurt them. But whether this was the cause of their actions or not, the Lord still wants to redeem the situation, thus, bringing glory to God.

Parents, I encourage you to stop asking *why*. It doesn't matter half as much as what God is going to do in your children's lives to bring them back to their senses. Nothing surprises God; He knows beforehand what is going to happen, and He already has a plan set in place to redeem the situation.

You may be wondering why God allowed these things to happen to your children. You may wonder why He didn't stop it because you know He has the power to do just that. You may have been praying for years and wonder why God hasn't answered your prayer. This could be an entire teaching in itself, so I will put it as simply as possible.

God gave everyone a free will, which He will not go against. Yes, He knew some would use that free will for bad. Why, then, did He give it to us knowing that some would use it to make ungodly decisions? Because He wanted us to love Him freely and not because we were forced to love Him. It's as if it was all worth it to Him to risk the possibility of some rejecting Him, if He could get others to love Him, just because they wanted to.

A good example of this concept is when my daughter was dating a man for months who loved her and wanted to marry her, but she did not love him. She told him so, but he didn't care; he still wanted to marry her. This was extreme selfishness on this man's part because he was going to try to force her to love him. He didn't know that he could never be happy with someone he had to force to love him. This is the same way God feels; He wants us to love Him

Introduction

because it is our desire, not because we are forced, and this is why He gave us a free will.

Parents, no matter what you may be going through, there is always hope with God! Look at Romans 15:13 again:

Now the God of hope fill you with all joy and peace in believing, that ye may abound in hope, through the power of the Holy Ghost.

Many people tend to believe that the word "hope" means that we are hoping that God will do something for us. This is not what it means. The Greek definition of *hope* is "a joyful and confident expectation of good." This is saying that because we trust in God to be faithful to our children in their times of struggle, we will be filled with joy and peace. Once we experience joy and peace, we can overflow in hope, which simply means we will now be confident of a great outcome.

It begins with believing. But we can't do this on our own. According to the above verse, it is through the power of the Holy Spirit that we will abound with hope. This hope is such a positive expectation that no one could change your mind about the good that will come. It may not happen overnight, but it will happen.

The following pages reveal Biblical principles from the Word of God to help us learn how to stand for our children in this day and age. It is our responsibility to do so.

I will be sharing personal stories of some problems my husband and I have dealt with, but there is one thing I want to make clear: some of the measures we took with our daughter may not be what God wants you to do. We get into trouble when we do the same thing others have done in a particular situation, when God had a totally different plan in place for us. We must make sure we hear directly from God before making a move. Of course, there are some Biblical principles that everyone should practice, but it's those personal instructions for your particular issue that may vary. He works according to our faith, and we are all at different levels of faith.

Introduction

But remember this: God is so good and loves your children even more than you do. Just watch what He can do. He won't let you down. No matter how bad it looks, there is hope! Nothing is too difficult for Him, the God of Hope.

At the end of each chapter, there will be a prayer that I encourage you to say out loud. These prayers are not meant to be the only ones you say, but it will help give you an idea of the way you should be praying. Take each prayer and expand upon it as you converse with your Heavenly Father who loves to hear from you!

PRAYER:
Father, I thank You for getting this book into my hands. I ask you, Holy Spirit, that you speak to me through these pages teaching me how to deal with_____.

I know that these problems are not from You, but believe that You are our answer. Our culture may be evil, but Your Word says that we are delivered from the evils of this present world, so I believe it. (Galatians 1:4)

Hope For Your Children

I believe that_____ is also delivered from this evil world and I choose to have a positive expectation of a good outcome in my child's life. I trust You, Lord, to show me clearly through these pages how to stand for_____.

In Jesus Name, Amen.

Chapter 1

They Belong to God

The earth is the Lord's, and the fulness thereof;
the world, and they that dwell therein.
Psalm 24:1

It all started going wrong when my daughter got her driver's license along with a job at a department store. It was there she met a group of ungodly people who were able to sway her from all that she had learned from us. She made her decision; her rebellion began by skipping school and breaking curfews.

One day I was approaching her bedroom. The door was closed; she wasn't home at the time and I wanted to search her room. As I put my hand on the door knob, the Lord spoke to me and said: "Take your hand off the door knob; turn around and trust Me. She belongs to Me."

I never really thought about it; if I belong to God, then my children also belong to Him. From that moment on, I began learning how to trust God. But that was nothing compared to what He spoke to us a few months later. God was speaking to my husband and me at the same time and said the same thing.

He told us to put her out of the house. While lying in bed that night, I questioned God about it. No matter which way I looked at it, I could not deny that I had heard from God. I was overwhelmed with peace.

We did as the Lord told us to do. We put all her belongings out on the front lawn, called her and told her to come get her things. Then we changed the locks on the doors which was heart-breaking for us, but all the while always remembering that she did not belong to us; she belonged to God.

Psalm 24:1 tells us clearly that everything and everyone belongs to the Lord. Also, Psalm 127:3

states: *Lo, children are an heritage of the Lord: and the fruit of the womb is his reward.* One of the meanings of the word *heritage* is "possession." Parents, according to these two verses, we *all* belong to the Lord.

God has entrusted our children to our care. It's called "stewardship." Stewardship is often associated with money and/or possessions. But it's much more than just assets. It's taking care of something we do not own. God is the owner of everything, including our children, and we are their caregivers with the responsibility to nurture, guide, and teach them the ways of God.

And ye shall teach them, your children, speaking of them when thou sittest in thine house, and when thou walkest by the way, when thou liest down, and when thou risest up. (Deuteronomy 11:19)

Many may think that I wasn't a good parent by not searching my daughter's room. One family member even told me that I was not a responsible parent by putting her out of the house. It may have looked like that in the natural, but I heard from God directly and that's all that mattered.

Recently, I heard a great story from my son-in-law's mother. Years ago when her children were very young, she was rushed to the hospital thinking she was having a heart attack. Her husband was extremely worried as it appeared that he would be losing his wife. She told me while in the hospital she started talking to God. She was worried about her children. She didn't want to die young because she wanted to fulfill God's plan for her which was raising her children.

God spoke to her and said, "Your children have nothing to do with you. They belong to Me and I will take care of them." This was news to her, but you know what it did? It freed her from worrying about what would happen to them and it also freed her to let them become who God created them to be as they got older.

Look at 1 Corinthians 4:7:

For who maketh thee to differ from another? ***and***

They Belong to God

what hast thou that thou didst not receive? now if thou didst receive it, why dost thou glory, as if thou hadst not received it?

I hear story after story of parents who unnecessarily take on the cares and burdens of their children as if they own them. It's right to teach them and guide them; it's right to correct them when they do wrong, and it's right to discipline them when it's appropriate. That's our job.

It is *not* our job to carry the burden with a heavy heart while trying to fix and control them. It's important that we understand this truth. It should be freeing to know that God is in charge of your children. It's up to Him to decide how He will work with them when they go their own way. We just have to trust Him to do it. I tell parents all the time that it's God's job to take care of our kids, and it's our job to trust God to do it.

If this is a new truth to you, then talk with your Heavenly Father and thank Him for revealing this truth. Then turn your children over to Him, trusting

Him to do what He so longs to do in their lives. He will take care of them because they belong to Him!

PRAYER:

Father, thank You for revealing the truth to me that _____ belongs to You.

I realize I have been carrying a burden I need not carry. I release _____ to You and by faith believe that You will take care of him/her because You love _____ even more than I do.

I trust You. In Jesus Name, Amen.

Chapter 2

Get Rid of Worry

Thou wilt keep him in perfect peace, whose mind is stayed on thee: because he trusteth in thee.

Isaiah 26:3

When dealing with an issue regarding our children, we, as parents, can experience such a wave of various emotions in just a short period of time.

For example, I know of many parents who have a child in prison. They are sad and unhappy about it, yet they are excited because the day is coming when their child will be released from prison. But, at the same time, that excitement turns into fear and uncertainty as they wonder what might happen when their child returns home. Will there be enough strength to resist the same temptations that led to prison in the first place? But then a sense of peace overwhelms them, knowing that even though their child is in prison, at least he or she is safe - such a flood of different emotions. If we aren't careful, those feelings can eventually control us.

There were so many emotions my husband and I experienced when we obeyed the Lord's direction to put our daughter out of the house. We certainly had peace and a sense of stability knowing God was taking care of her. At the same time we felt rejected, heartbroken, uncertain, and even a bit resentful and irritated toward her. We felt tired and useless, but yet we were thankful to God and comforted by the Holy Spirit. We even spent some time condemning and blaming ourselves, thinking we may have done something to cause this nightmare.

The emotions that seemed to grip me the most were worry and fear. For the next three months our daughter was living in an airport hanger with her boyfriend. You may say that it was understandable why I was worried, and that may be true; however, I learned over the years that I have a right to experience peace and joy in the midst of struggles.

I learned how to fight negative emotions with the Word of God. I realized I didn't have to deal with discouragement, uncertainty, loneliness, frustration, anger, fear, worry, anxiety, etc. I learned I could remain in peace by focusing on God and His Word and standing for what He says is rightfully mine.

When Jesus died on the cross, He died for *everything*, not just forgiveness of sins. He took all our sins and all the guilt and condemnation that goes with sinning (Matt. 1:21, Romans 8:1); He took our sicknesses and diseases (Isaiah 53:4-5); He took our poverty. (2 Cor. 8:9) He also delivered us from all demonic hold, fear, worry, anxiety, confusion, addictions, loneliness, pain, and grief. (Luke 8:33) If Jesus took all these things onto Himself, then we do not have to carry them. This is great news!

I believe we, as parents, think a big part of parenting is to worry. We believe it's our way of caring. We seem to worry about everything from the foods our children eat, to the friends they have, to the teachers that were assigned to them. God forbid we hear something negative about a teacher and then find out our child will be in that class the following year! There's no condemnation here; I did it all.

We worry about their grades, if others are treating them right, if they are getting enough sleep, if they are happy or not. If we see a sniffle, we worry about them getting sick. We even worry about what other people think if we don't worry.

As our children get older, we continue to worry: Will they be good drivers? Are their friends good drivers? Will they skip classes in high school? Will they choose wrong friends? Will they use self-control when needed, or will they try illegal drugs? - full of worry and care. This is living as if our children belong to us, but they belong to God, as we spoke about in Chapter One.

If you want to be free from worry, you must first recognize that you *do* worry. Some parents are so used to worrying that they can't even see it. I remember years ago someone accused me of being filled with fear. I denied it right to his face and was angry that this person would say that to me.

But when he left our home that evening, I asked the Lord, "Am I filled with fear?" The Lord told me, "Yes, you are full of fear." The point is that I checked with God; He, in His love for me, revealed the truth. This opened up the door for me to learn how to be free from fear.

I encourage you to go to your Heavenly Father and ask Him to reveal to you the areas in your life where there may be fear and worry. He loves you and wants you free from these destructive emotions.

The title of this book is *Hope for Your Children*. As we discussed in the Introduction, hope is the "confident expectation of good." Worry and fear (they go hand in hand) is expecting or anticipating the worst-case scenario. Worry is the opposite of hope. We cannot expect good and anticipate the worst at the same time. Which will you choose: worry or hope? It *is* a choice.

You may say that fear and worry are a result of your circumstances. The circumstances obviously *lead* to worry and fear. Although you may have an initial emotion of fear flood your body, it doesn't have to remain there. Fear and worry begin in the mind, which is the only place the devil can attempt to lie to us. He rules by deception; he is the father of lies and will speak those lies to your mind until you believe them.

However, because the Bible says the devil has already been destroyed through the cross (Hebrews 2:14), you don't have to believe those lies. He wants you so upset about your children that you become incapable of fulfilling the plan God has for you on a daily basis.

Also, the devil wants you filled with worry and care to the point of making you physically sick.

My husband and I have a long time friend who took the care of his children onto himself since they were very young. His whole life was centered around them. He worked very hard to put them into the best schools. As they got older, he purchased various businesses for them so they could manage them; he gave them several opportunities because he wanted them to succeed in every way. He worked around the clock to make sure his family had the best of everything.

Today his children are doctors and lawyers, but their father is a mess. Because of all the stress he brought onto himself over the years, he is now facing a life-threatening disease. Stress may begin with our emotions, but ends up affecting our physical bodies in a negative way, if we don't deal with it.

There's nothing wrong with us, as parents, helping our children succeed in life; we should help them, but never to the point of taking the care and burden of it all onto ourselves. This is a lack of trust in God. We just do not believe that He will take care of them, and we think we can do a much better job than He could or would be willing to do.

The next few chapters will teach you how to combat fear and worry concerning your children.

Let's begin to deal with it.

PRAYER:

Father, I realize that worry is a lack of trust in You. Reveal to me areas in my life where there is worry and fear. (Wait for God to reveal them.)

Lord, thank You for showing me where fear and worry exist in my life. I repent for worrying about_____. I realize I have been believing the lies of the enemy. Please continue to show me when I am carrying burdens I should not be carrying.

I make the decision to trust You to take care of _____ much better than I can. Thank You for doing just that!

In Jesus Name, Amen.

Chapter 3

A Simple First Step

Be careful for nothing; but in every thing by prayer and supplication with thanksgiving let your requests be made known unto God. And the peace of God, which passeth all understanding, shall keep your hearts and minds through Christ Jesus.

Philippians 4:6-7

In looking at the above scripture, God tells us not to worry or be anxious. He doesn't just wave His magic wand and the worry disappears. It's up to *us* to not worry or fear.

In fact, to be *careful for nothing* means that we should be totally care-free! God would not tell us to be worry free, if it weren't possible. It's the grace of God that has made a way for us to stay in peace without a care.

God's Word is so clear. In this passage, as with so many others, He doesn't only tell us what *not* to do, He then tells us what *to do* followed by the result. It's very simple and easy to understand. I love what Bible teacher, Andrew Wommack, says quite often: "The Bible is so easy to understand that you have to have someone help you to misunderstand it!"

Continuing with this verse, God tells us how to be free from worry and fear:

...but in every thing by prayer and supplication with thanksgiving, let your requests be made known unto God. (Phil. 4: 6)

Prayer should begin with honoring God for who He is through praise and thanksgiving. No matter what our problems may be, we should bring them to the Lord with praise and with thankful hearts first:

Enter into his gates with thanksgiving, and into his courts with praise: be thankful unto him, and bless

A Simple First Step

his name. (Psalms 100:4)

You may not feel like praising God, but this is where faith comes in. Hebrews 13:15 tells us to *offer the sacrifice of praise to God continually*. This means praising Him even when we can't see His goodness and when we think He has forgotten us.

Praising God during these times is a sacrifice on our part because we see nothing happening in the natural for which to praise Him. But by praising Him in the midst of the storm, we are activating our faith and bringing pleasure to God. Hebrews 11:6 says: *But without faith, it is impossible to please him...*

Praising God also increases our confidence in seeing the goodness of God manifested in the situation.

The word *supplication* means "making a request." Although every answer to every problem we could ever have was provided for us at the cross, and although God knows our needs before we ask Him, He still wants us to come to Him and make our requests known to Him. It's part of having a relationship with Him.

Many Christians believe that they are supposed to ask God over and over again for the same thing until He comes through. This is incorrect. Asking the Lord more than once is unbelief. You didn't believe He would do it the first time you asked, so you are asking again. God can't work where there is unbelief:

And he did not many mighty works there because of their unbelief. (Matt. 13:58)

God only works in the realm of faith. It is faith to believe that He heard you the first time and that the answer is on its way.

A good example would be if my children asked me for $5.00 and I gave it to them. With the $5.00 still in their hands, they ask me for $5.00. I already answered them the first time. It wouldn't make me feel too good if they didn't recognize that I already met their needs. It's the same with God. Trust that He hears your request and know that it is done.

What follows supplication is *thanksgiving*. This

A Simple First Step

act is powerful when you thank God for answering your prayer requests before you actually see it.

We all remember the story of the Israelites crossing the Red Sea. (Exodus, Chapter 14) After Moses delivered them out of Egypt, Pharaoh's heart was once again hardened, so he pursued them. The Egyptian army came behind the Israelites who stood between them and the Red Sea. They were frightened and began complaining to Moses for taking them out of Egypt in the first place.

God told Moses to lift his rod, and as he did, the sea parted and the Israelites crossed to the other side, but then the waters covered the enemy. Chapter 15 begins with the song Moses and the children of Israel sang because of this great victory.

This all sounds admirable, and, yes, we should thank God when we experience victory in our lives, but where the Israelites went wrong was they should have been thanking and praising God *before* the sea was parted. It was natural for them to praise Him *after* the victory, but it would have been FAITH to praise Him *before* it.

Now faith is the substance of things hoped for, the evidence of things not seen. (Hebrews 11:1)

When we give thanks before we actually see anything happening, we are letting God know that we believe He is on the scene bringing the answer. This is what pleases the Lord.

Let's look at 1 Thessalonians 5:18:

In every thing give thanks: for this is the will of God in Christ Jesus concerning you.

This scripture has been misunderstood by many Christians. First of all, we are not to give thanks *for* everything, but *in* everything. There is a difference.

During those years dealing with my daughter and her decisions, I never once gave thanks *for* any of it. But I did give thanks *in* all of it. Why would I thank God for evil? I didn't.

I thanked Him because He was still on the throne knowing everything we were going through and knowing that His will would be done in my daughter's life because that is what I desired. Although she was living in an airport hanger, I thanked God for protecting her from all harm; I thanked Him for His mercy on her and for His love for her. I thanked Him because He would never let me down.

But here is where some really miss it. Where it says *this is the will of God*, most interpret it to mean that whatever trial you are facing, it is the will of God, but that is incorrect. What it is really saying is that *this* (giving thanks) is the will of God. So, if for no other reason, we are to give thanks just because it is His will for us to give thanks.

Once you begin thanking God for what you can't see yet in the physical realm, then according to Philippians 4:7, you will experience the peace of God which will preserve your heart and mind through the process.

Parents, you want this peace; you need this peace! It's what will carry you through. It's when you are at peace that you will be able to hear from God. He wants to lead and guide you in your difficulties, but you won't be able to hear Him if your heart and mind is in turmoil because of worry and fear.

The steps are easy: Praise and worship God; ask Him to reveal to you where you may be worrying; lay out your prayer requests before Him once, and thank Him continually for answering your prayers. You will begin to experience His peace:

And the peace of God, which passeth all understanding, shall keep your hearts and minds through Christ Jesus. (Phil. 4:7)

This peace is so supernatural that you couldn't feel fear even if you tried, and you certainly won't be able to explain it to others. It's God's peace, and it's for you!

PRAYER: (Begin by praising and worshiping God) *Father, thank You for showing me the areas in my life where I am worried and fearful. Thank You for showing me that I do not need to have a care about_____.*

A Simple First Step

According to Philippians 4:6-7, I bring my requests before You. (Lay out your petitions.)

Father, I thank You for answering my deepest desires. No matter what it looks like I trust that You are actively working in _____'s life by leading, guiding, and protecting _____.

I thank You for Your peace that passes all understanding and that I am able to hear Your voice to know what to do or not to do.

In Jesus Name, Amen.

Chapter 4
Cast Your Care

Humble yourselves therefore under the mighty hand of God, that he may exalt you in due time: Casting all your care upon him; for he careth for you.

1 Peter 5:6-7

Have you ever been on the telephone with someone and before hanging up, they said to you, "Take care"? Many people have said that to me, but I must admit that for years I ended my conversations saying the same thing to others.

What people are really telling you is to take cares onto yourself. This is not a blessing phrase and it does not line up with what the Bible teaches, at all. You may think this is just a minor thing, but there is tremendous power in the words we speak.

As we read in the previous chapter, we are not to have any cares. We are supposed to be care-free, so telling someone to "take care" is the opposite of what God calls us to do.

So now whenever someone tells me to "take care," I hang up the phone and say what the Bible says: "I do not take the care; God takes my care!"

The Bible tells us in 1 Peter 5 (see beginning of chapter) that we are to cast our care onto Him because He cares for us. It's God's job to take our care; He wants to because He loves and cares for us, and this is why it should be easy for us to do so.

Casting our care is a sign of humility. Verse 6 tells us to humble ourselves and verse 7 tells us how – *casting our care onto the Lord*. To take matters into our own hands in any given situation is once again unbelief. We just don't believe God can handle our problems. We think we can do a better job than He can. We do not trust Him to do it right. We act as if we know the inner hearts of our children better than He does. Humility is admitting that God knows more than we know. But it's our pride that says otherwise.

Our part as parents is to trust God – not ourselves, or our own ideas, and as we yield to Him, He will lead and direct us:

Trust in the Lord with all thine heart; and lean not unto thine own understanding. In all thy ways acknowledge him, and he shall direct thy paths. (Proverbs 3:5-6)

At one point, during those three months while our daughter was living in an airport hanger with her boyfriend, she called me and asked me to bring her a coat because it was a very cold day. I stayed very strong and spoke very calmly telling her that I was sorry, but that I would not bring her a coat. The grace of God was obvious during that phone call, as He was giving me His ability to do what I needed to do at the time. God is so good.

I do not intend to minimize your problems with your children, but no matter what you may be going through, God's grace is sufficient for you. He gives you the ability to not fall apart, but to stand strong in what He tells you to do.

This is what God told the Apostle Paul. Paul was severely persecuted by many people because of his message, so he asked God three times to take this problem away. God told him, "My grace is sufficient for you." He was telling Paul that he (Paul) had the ability to continue to do what God called him to do even in the midst of major persecution.

We have this same grace and thank God for it. In fact, during the trials with my daughter, I was working at a local church of about 500 people and there wasn't one person who could tell I had a problem in my life. God gave me His ability to continue the plan He had for me, even in the midst of some serious problems.

Our daughter returned home at the end of those three months, pregnant. What a bitter-sweet moment! We were sad because of the way she chose to do it, but glad because God created this child with a special plan in place for him.

Before my grandson was born, she decided to get married. My husband and I both knew that she shouldn't marry this person. There were many reasons for that, but it was what they planned to do, regardless of what we might have said.

Once again I had mixed emotions because getting married would "make it right." But at the same time, I knew he was not a good person to marry. We did the best we could by giving them a nice wedding and loving them through this time.

I was learning how to cast my care. What I really wanted to do was to blow up at her and her boyfriend, shake them, and forbid them to marry. It was a real battle between my natural senses and what the Spirit of God was telling me, which was to remain silent.

My daughter was married and about three months pregnant when the Lord spoke to me. He told me to go over to their apartment every day (they had their own place by this time) and pray for the baby. I wrestled with it because I did not want to be anywhere near her husband or in that apartment because nothing seemed right. I suspected a long road ahead of nothing but trouble.

My husband told me that if I could minister to hundreds of children each week, which is what I was doing at the time, then I could at least pray for our future grandchild everyday. So I did; my grandson, who is now fifteen years old, is blessed, blessed, blessed!

But notice that as I was casting my care, there were still some things the Lord told me to do. I was to pray for the baby and his mom everyday. I was doing my part, while the Lord took the rest of the responsibility to bring my daughter to where she is today. I had no idea how He would do it; in fact, it was none of my business how He intended on changing her. It was just my job to hear, obey, and trust.

I wasn't perfect at this. There were times that I would have a good handle on casting my care onto the Lord, only to find myself taking the care back. It was wearing me out inside.

But there was a reason why I took the care back. It began in my mind. The next chapter will reveal the power of our thoughts.

PRAYER:
Father, thank You for showing me that I have been taking the care of _____ onto myself. I realize I have kept You out of so many decisions. I am sorry. I make the decision to cast my care onto You because I know that You love me and care for me and my family.

I trust You with_____. I thank You for Your grace that empowers me to continue doing what You have called me to do while resting in Your ability to take care of _____.

In Jesus Name, Amen.

Chapter 5
Think Right!

Finally, brethren, whatsoever things are true, whatsoever things are honest, whatsoever things are just, whatsoever things are pure, whatsoever things are lovely, whatsoever things are of good report; if there be any virtue, and if there be any praise, think on these things.

Philippians 4:8

Years ago, when my children were in elementary school, they would tell me that the best part of their school day was recess. They looked forward to it all morning, anticipating the fun they would have outside.

I, myself, have seen the excitement of children

as the bell rang, the doors opened, and they would charge to the playground to begin their fantasy play time. They would play for hours if they could! When the bell rang to go back into the classroom, they were somewhat sad that it was over, but at the same time happy with what they felt they accomplished outside.

Our mind can be the devil's playground. He waits for just the right time, and then charges our minds with an onslaught of lies that stir up negative emotions such as fear, worry, guilt or shame.

When our daughter was skipping classes in high school, some of our family members actually told us that we were not good parents because we didn't drive her to school everyday and walk her into her tenth grade classroom. (Like she couldn't leave after that?)

As I mentioned in an earlier chapter, they also made it clear that we were wrong in putting her out of the house and that she never would have become pregnant if we hadn't. Just for the record, Kristin was determined to have a child no matter where she lived.

The devil took these opportunities to try and make us think that our daughter was making wrong decisions based on the mistakes we had made in raising her. He wanted us to feel guilty and condemned. If we would have taken his bait, we would have felt badly about ourselves which could have led to depression and physical illness, not to mention dealing with offense within our family. The devil never gives up, and he doesn't play fair. Unfortunately, most parents do not even recognize what's happening.

How can we tell when our thoughts are wrong? Our emotions tell us. When we experience the emotion of fear, it's a sign that we are not thinking according to the Word of God, which would be a wrong thought.

Emotions do not emerge as a result of our circumstances; they emerge because of *what we are thinking of at the time.* It would be wise to pause the moment fear raises its ugly head and ask yourself,

"What was I thinking that led to this fear?" Once we recognize the thought, we can then do something about it.

We need to make sure every thought we have lines up with the Word of God. For example, your teenager just received his or her license and borrows your car for the evening. Rather than worry about the safety of your child, you can turn your thoughts to Psalm 91 and read out loud and meditate on verses 11 and 12:

For he shall give his angels charge over thee, to keep thee in all thy ways. They shall bear thee up in their hands, lest thou dash thy foot against a stone.

Start thanking God for His angels that are with your children and that the angels will hold them in their hands if any harm tries to come to them. This, parents, is faith. It is exalting the Word of God above any natural possibilities. It is your response to what God already provided by Grace, which is protection for your children.

Thoughts are powerful, whether positive or

negative. Almost everything begins in our thought life: our decisions, behaviors and the words we speak. What we choose to think can determine the outcome of our circumstances. Eventually those thoughts, if entertained long enough, will be spoken out of our mouth and that's when we will begin to see the fruit of our words play out in our lives.

As I said earlier, our thoughts are a direct link to our physical health. We first must understand that we were never made for fear. We were created in love and by Love, Himself.

Look at what happens when fear, which begins in the mind, begins to grip us. Thousands of chemicals within our bodies go into disarray which leads to a chemical imbalance. These chemicals are trying to locate the fear, but it can't because we are wired for love only, not fear. So they go into chaos, causing physical problems in our body. This is how powerful our thoughts are.

On the other hand, if we think of things that are good and lovely and pure, then our bodies experience the peace and good health God intended for us.

I remember in Kristin's first year of marriage, they offered to take care of a friend's dog – a pit bull. So here was my beautiful one-year-old grandson walking around in the same house with a pit bull!

I realize there are many who say that these dogs are not vicious if they are correctly trained, and that may be true, but every horrific story that I have ever heard involved a pit bull. You can imagine the fear that was trying to destroy me.

How did I handle it? I never said a word to my daughter about yet another unwise decision; if I did, we would have had a very big blow out. Strife is never good; it causes confusion and invites the devil into your situation big time.

For where envying and strife is, there is confusion and every evil work. (James 3:16)

I didn't talk to my daughter, but I talked to God. I voiced my concern, asked Him to take care of it and then thanked Him for doing it. I thanked Him for

Think Right!

doing it everyday because the devil was having a blast "playing at recess" in my mind.

Jesus, Himself, struggled with thoughts. In the Gospel of John, Chapter 13, Jesus had the opportunity to become fearful of what was going to happen to Him:

Now before the feast of the passover, when Jesus knew that his hour was come that he should depart out of this world unto the Father, having loved his own which were in the world, he loved them unto the end. And supper being ended, the devil having now put into the heart of Judas Iscariot, Simon's son, to betray him; (vv.1-2)

Jesus began thinking that His time was getting closer and that He would be leaving this world and going to His Father. I'm sure as He thought about the suffering ahead of Him, He had an opportunity to become fearful.

He continued to think about His disciples. He not only loved them dearly, but also knew that their faith was just not strong enough to endure what was about to happen. He had the opportunity to become worried for them.

After supper, He began to think of the one who would betray Him. Jesus' thoughts were declining. Remember, He was operating in His humanity at the time, so He experienced things that we experience. But look what He does in verses 3 & 4:

Jesus knowing that the Father had given all things into his hands, and that he was come from God, and went to God; He riseth from supper, and laid aside his garments; and took a towel, and girded himself.

He could have become saddened over one of His own, who was preparing to betray Him and hand Him over to those who wanted to kill Him. Instead, Jesus pulled Himself off the path of depression and fear by reminding Himself of who He was in the Father, that He had all things given to Him such as grace, power and authority, and that He came from His Father and was going back to Him. Because of this, He was able to continue to do what His Father called Him to do, which was to be a servant. He began to wash the

Think Right!

feet of His disciples.

Jesus changed His thinking on purpose. Those thoughts didn't just dissipate – He had to replace those thoughts with what His Father said about Him. As parents, we can and should do the same thing.

There was so much turmoil in Kristin's marriage; we had to continually change our thinking to what God said about the situation. It wasn't easy at times, but it allowed us to remain positive and at peace as we continued to serve Him.

Meditate on who you want your children to become. See them with your heart as healed, joyful, happy, content, and free. This is the way God sees them. What can be somewhat helpful is to find pictures of your children during a happy moment in their life and put those pictures on your mirror, refrigerator, or anywhere you can see them regularly. This is seeing them the way you expect them to be once again. It brings great confidence as you are encouraged by what the Lord already says about your child.

PRAYER:

Thank You for showing me that I have a choice as to what I allow my mind to dwell on. I recognize that the enemy can fill my mind with lies of fear and worry. I make a decision to think on whatever is true, honest, pure and lovely.

Help me to recognize immediately when my thoughts are not according to Your Word so that I can replace them with words of life. Thank You.

In Jesus Name, Amen.

Chapter 6
Speak Right!

Death and life are in the power of the tongue: and they that love it shall eat the fruit thereof.
Proverbs 18:21

One of the things we learned while dealing with our daughter's decisions was the importance of the things we spoke. Words have tremendous power!

As we covered in the last chapter, everything starts with our thought life. When we become aware of our thoughts, we can actually change them. But if we let our negative or fearful thoughts continue, they will eventually come out of our mouths. We give life to our thoughts when we begin to speak them.

Therefore take no thought, saying, What shall we eat? or, What shall we drink? or, Wherewithal shall we be clothed? (Matt. 6:31)

Owning our words is a reality and can be a danger zone because according to Proverbs 18:21, *Death and life are in the power of the tongue: and they that love it shall eat the fruit thereof.* Simply put, we will have what we say!

Although most people would say that the primary purpose of words is for communication, this is not correct. Yes, we communicate with words, but the primary purpose is for the release of creative power. When we speak, we create. It's that simple. God created this beautiful world through His spoken word.

Look at Proverbs 18:21 again. The word *power* means "direction." So death and life are in the *direction* our tongue decides to take, and we will eat the fruit of it. It's our choice.

In the book of Numbers, Chapter 14, Moses delivered the Israelites from their oppression in

Speak Right!

Egypt and was leading them through the wilderness to the Promised Land. Things were getting difficult, and they began murmuring against Moses and their situation. They **said** they would rather have died in Egypt or the wilderness (v. 2) and it would be better for them to go back (v. 3). God's anger began to flare up (v. 12) and Moses interceded for them. God said to Moses, *I have pardoned **according to thy word*** (v. 20) and did not smite them. Notice that God *did* as Moses *said*.

In verse 28, God had a message for the Israelites, Say unto them, *As truly as I live, saith the Lord,* ***as ye have spoken*** *in mine ears, so will I do to you.* They **spoke** that they either wanted to go back to Egypt or die in the wilderness; God gave them what they spoke. Other than Joshua and Caleb, no one entered the Promised Land; they all died in the wilderness. We will have what we say!

In dealing with rebellious children, there will always be a temptation to speak negative things about them: "She is a very selfish person." "He is such an ungrateful child." "He is so greedy, never satisfied and always wants more." In my daughter Kristin's case, I remember saying quite often, "She doesn't take *no* for an answer."

The problem with speaking this way was that she continued *not* taking *no* for an answer! As long as I kept saying those words, she never took *no* for an answer, until, one day, I changed my speech life. It was only then that Kristin began to change.

How did I change my speech life? Let's look at Romans 4:17:

...even God, who quickeneth the dead, and calleth those things which be not as though they were.

Rather than speaking what she was, I began speaking what I wanted her to be, but as if it was already done. This is important: according to the above scripture, if God calls things that are not as though they *already* were, then we should do the same. This is how to walk by faith and not by sight. No matter what I saw in front of me, I ignored it and made sure that I spoke the opposite.

Speak Right!

You may say that I wasn't in reality, but in God's Kingdom, it *is* reality. Rather than saying my daughter never took *no* for an answer, I would say, "Kristin is an obedient child and wants to please us. Our daughter respects our decisions as parents; she is blessed and obedient." Not only does speaking like this encourage us, as parents, but it also agrees with what God says about our children and ultimately changes the situation.

In Matthew, Chapter 5, Jesus is speaking to His disciples. This was the beginning of His ministry, and He was teaching them fundamental truths of His Kingdom.

I was always amazed that in verse 13, Jesus called His disciples the "salt of the earth" and in verse 14 He called them the "light of the world." The disciples had not been with Jesus very long and had just begun to learn some things they never heard before, yet Jesus still saw them as salt and light!

As rebellious as your children may seem to be, our Heavenly Father still sees them as salt and light;

He still sees them as saved, protected, delivered, healthy, and restored. This is faith, parents. You must see your children as God sees them.

You may not feel like you believe it at first, but that's okay. Just say these truths out loud. Call your son or daughter saved, delivered, protected, healthy and restored in Jesus' Name. A confidence will rise up in you, and you will actually believe and see them as such.

My husband, Al, and I were very careful not to speak anything negative regarding Kristin to other people. As I mentioned earlier, my co-workers did not even know anything was going on with our family. This is the way it should be.

However, we shared everything with each other. We shared our anger, our disappointments, and our frustrations. We didn't have too many good things to say about Kristin's husband, either.

The Lord showed us that it was good that we weren't talking to others about our trials, but He also showed us that it wasn't wise to talk about it with each other, either. I thought for sure it would be okay to talk with Al about the situation, and it *was* right to do so when decisions had to be made, but we were just downright complaining to each other. Here is what God wanted us to know: It's not *who* we share with; it's *what* we share.

We could be talking out loud to ourselves, but if they are not words of life, then it is destructive. God was showing us that we needed to be careful what we spoke all the time no matter to whom we were speaking.

Let's talk about the seriousness of murmuring and complaining. Look at Exodus 16:2:

And the whole congregation of the children of Israel murmured against Moses and Aaron in the wilderness.

The original Hebrew meaning of the word *murmur* is "to stop, to stay permanently, to abide, be left, lie all night, to lodge, to remain." This meaning should convince us all to stop our complaining because when we complain, we remain in the trial.

As long as we kept complaining about our daughter, she remained there; the situation never changed. It was only once we stopped complaining that things changed for the better. Complaining has the same effect on everyone all the time.

Do yourself a favor as a parent and stop complaining about your children. If you don't stop, you will remain in your situation with them. In a sense, you are telling God He's not answering your requests quickly enough. He is working, parents; trust Him.

PRAYER:
Lord, forgive me for complaining and for all the words of death and despair that I have spoken regarding_____.

Thank You, Lord, for showing me that my words have creative power. From this moment on, I choose to speak words of life and victory and believe that circumstances will change for the better in our family. Thank You.

In Jesus Name, Amen.

Chapter 7

Pray Right!

Therefore I say unto you, What things soever ye desire,
when ye pray, believe that ye receive them,
and ye shall have them.

Mark 11:24

Toward the end of a recent Bible study I was attending, I overheard two women talking about their children. One was a grandmother who had been praying for her grandson, and the other was a mom who had been praying for her son.

It seemed that both of these children had been demonstrating behavior that was not acceptable to either of them. It was obvious they were concerned about them. I heard one of them say, "I don't know what to do any more; I keep praying and things keep getting worse." At that point, I decided to walk over to their table and talk with them.

They had legitimate concerns for both of these boys, who apparently decided that they didn't have to obey rules any longer and were making their own unwise daily decisions.

What I quickly realized was that these women had no idea how to pray correctly. Their prayer life was fear-based and consisted of murmuring, complaining and begging, which demonstrates a total lack of faith and trust in God. I ministered to them for just a few moments which brought them hope. Thank You, Jesus.

It is my belief that there are two major areas that are hindering our prayers for our children. Let me illustrate: Some time ago, my husband, Al, had a vision of God standing in the center of thousands of people who were all praying. Their prayers were going upward toward the face of God, but their prayers passed right by Him and continued in an upright position. God wasn't answering them; it was as if He couldn't even hear them.

Al asked the Lord to show him the meaning of the vision. God showed him that His children were asking Him for things He had already given them, and they were asking Him to do things He had told them to do.

Have you ever prayed, "Dear God, please protect my son; Lord, please forgive my daughter; Bless my child today; Give me Your peace; Help me as a parent not to worry; Take away my fears; God, take the devil away from my child; Give my child faith?"

I prayed this way when problems first occurred with Kristin and it got me nowhere. I didn't understand why things weren't changing; in fact, problems appeared to be escalating. I wanted desperately to know why my prayers weren't being answered.

The first problem with these types of prayers is that we are asking God to give us something that He has already given us.

Unfortunately, many Christians do not know who they are in Christ and what they have been given, resulting in trying to get God to do something for us that we think He hasn't done yet. This is incorrect. God has done absolutely everything He will ever do! He moved ONCE and for all, according to Hebrews 10:10. It was all done at the cross 2,000 years ago.

The Greek word *sozo* has been translated to mean "save" or "saved" which refers to salvation. But it also translates to "physical healing" (See Mark 5:23, Acts 14:8-10) and to "be made whole," referring to healing in every way—physically and emotionally. (Luke 8:50) The word also applies to deliverance from demons. (Luke 8:36) And 2 Corinthians 8:9 makes it clear that we are redeemed from poverty.

As we read in Chapter Two, salvation encompasses everything—forgiveness of sins, physical healing, deliverance, prosperity, wholeness, and completeness. Yet, we keep asking God for these things as if we don't have them, but we *do* have them! He can't answer prayers He's already answered, and He can't say *no* when He's already said *yes*!

Pray Right!

The Word of God is full of promises and they all belong to us. This is great news. There is nothing we could do to deserve them; we will never deserve them; this is what Grace is all about. What God wants us to do is to believe those promises and stand on them:

For all the promises of God in him are yea, and in him Amen, unto the glory of God by us. (2 Cor. 1:20)

We just need to apply our faith to allow the things that have been given to us by His grace to be released in our lives.

So rather than praying that God would protect your children, thank Him that His angels have been given charge over them. (Psalm 91:11) Rather than asking God to be with your children, thank Him that He never leaves them or forsakes them. (Hebrews 13:5) Instead of asking God to forgive your children, thank Him that He has forgiven their sins. (Hebrews 10:12) Rather than asking Him to bless your children, thank Him that they are blessed with all spiritual blessings. (Ephesians 1:3) Finally, instead of asking

Him for peace for your children, thank Him that the peace of God that passes all understanding is guarding their hearts and minds. (Philippians 4:7)

You may be thinking that none of this is true as far as your children are concerned, but it *is* true according to what God says about them. We need to agree with God!

You may find it hard to believe these truths at the beginning, but the more you claim them out loud, the more confidence you will gain in the fact that God is working. You will become more and more assured of this, which will bring you great peace. You will eventually believe what you are saying. Why? Because by speaking God's Word, you are renewing your mind to truth, which will transform you and change any situation:

And be not conformed to this world: but be ye transformed by the renewing of your mind, that ye may prove what is that good, and acceptable, and perfect, will of God. (Romans 12:2)

As we discussed in Chapter Three, according to

Pray Right!

Philippians 4:6 and 7, you can make your requests known to God. Once you do, then you need to know that your prayer was answered. It may not seem like God heard your prayer, but He did; it just takes time.

We can see this in Mark, Chapter 11, when Jesus cursed the fig tree: *no man eat fruit of thee hereafter for ever.* (v. 14) The moment He spoke to the tree the roots began to die, but it wasn't yet visible. It wasn't until the next day that the disciples saw the fig tree dried up from the roots. (v. 21)

Once Jesus spoke to the fig tree, it seemed as though He really believed it was done. There is no record of Jesus wondering if His prayer worked, or praying more than once. He just continued on with His ministry, so it was no surprise to Him when the tree was dried up the following morning.

Jesus wants to get to the root of your children's hearts, and He is using every wrong decision they make to bring them closer to Him. This can take some time, so during this time of waiting and expecting, you need to claim God's promises from His

Word. It is these very promises that will make and keep you strong in the midst of the battle. The trial, itself, will not make you strong as some believe; battles wear us out. It's His promises in the midst of the battle that keep us going. Hallelujah!

In the next chapter, we will take a look at the second major hindrance to answered prayer.

PRAYER:
Thank You, Lord, for revealing to me that the things I have been praying for have already been answered by You. Thank You for the cross. Thank You that I can and will stand on your promises regarding _____.

Continue to give me revelation knowledge on all that was accomplished 2000 years ago.

In Jesus Name, Amen.

Chapter 8

Take Your Authority!

For the weapons of our warfare are not carnal, but mighty through God to the pulling down of strong holds.
2 Corinthians 10:4

In the last chapter, we discovered one way that our prayers might be hindered. This chapter will reveal the second reason why I believe we don't see answers to our prayers.

My husband and I have been in ministry for many years, and we have had the privilege of teaching Christians who they are in Christ, what they have in Him, and how to use what they have been given.

The one thing that we notice is that many Christians, although walking with the Lord and some being in ministry themselves, know very little to almost nothing about the authority they have been given in Christ. Some declare that they have authority, but they never use it. I believe this is the second hindrance to our prayers being answered. We are asking God to do something He told us to do, when we already have been given His authority to do it.

Scripture is clear that the authority that was taken from Adam and Eve because of their sin was restored back to us when Jesus defeated the devil on the cross. Today we use that authority by faith.

As new covenant believers, we have dominion over much more than just the earth. (Genesis 1:28-30) We have control over ourselves and any situation that pertains to us, and we have control over the demonic realm.

Ephesians 1 tells us that we have the same power that raised Christ Jesus from the dead. Because of this, all principalities and powers are under our feet. (Eph. 1:19-22) Jesus, Himself, is living inside of us, and with Jesus comes everything else. We have everything we will ever need because He *is* everything we will ever need.

There are many whom some would call "control freaks." They love to be in control. They love to take charge. Some are more aggressive than others, but we all have some of that "take charge" in us. There's a desire to control meetings, personal conversations, decisions, and so forth.

What we don't realize is that we actually have all the control we need because God has given it to us! We have control over every area of our lives, but this control is not to be used selfishly.

Whenever we are in a conversation, and we feel we must have the last word, even with our children, this kind of control is completely selfish and void of God. It does not glorify God at all, but only feeds our carnal flesh. It is true that our children should respect us by not arguing with us, but this book is about helping you, the parent, deal with things like this in a Godly way.

I recall arguing with my daughter many times. As time went on, I felt I was just losing every battle. No matter what I told her, she ignored it and did what pleased her at the moment. I felt I was losing strength; even my voice was fading at times. After a while, it seemed like I really didn't mean what I was saying. I felt so helpless.

But praise God, in the midst of it all, when I was at my weakest, He was at His strongest. What I didn't realize at the time was that His strength was already in me!

Paul said in 2 Corinthians 12:10 that when he was weak, then he was strong. He knew that even in the weakest moments of his life, God was strong in him. If Paul could say this after everything he had been through, then so can we.

As we saw earlier in this chapter, Ephesians 1 tells us that we have the same power living in us that raised Jesus from the dead, which means God's strength is in us no matter what we may feel like.

The control, or authority that God has given us

Take Your Authority!

is to be used for one purpose only: to glorify God on this earth by bringing attention to Him, so that others will follow Him. We bring attention to Him by the victory people witness in our daily lives.

As far as dealing with your children, you need to understand when and how to use your authority. Yes, there are some practical things that you can do. I can't tell you how many times I took the car keys away from my daughter. But there is a much better way.

It was important for me to understand that my daughter was not my enemy. It sure looked as if she was; she disobeyed almost everything I told her to do or not to do. When I began to take it all so personally, the Lord revealed to me who the real enemy was.

In Matthew, Chapter 16, Jesus is telling His disciples that He would suffer and be killed at the hands of the religious leaders. Peter, one of his disciples, would not accept it:

Then Peter took him, and began to rebuke him, saying Be it far from thee, Lord: this shall not be unto thee. But he turned, and said unto Peter, Get thee behind me, Satan: thou art an offence unto me: for thou savourest not the things that be of God, but those that be of men. (vv.22-23)

Although Jesus was looking directly at Peter, He wasn't talking to Peter; He was rebuking the devil who spoke through Peter. Peter was not the enemy of Jesus; the devil was.

This is huge. Anyone who appears to be our enemy is not our real enemy. Your children are not your enemy.

Our enemy is the devil, himself. He is relentless in creating fear and worry and offense which leads to strife within the family. Look again at what strife does:

For where envying and strife is, there is confusion and every evil work. (James 3:16)

Parents, you cannot afford to have strife within your family. The devil is continually looking for an opening into your life and the lives of your children.

One of the main ways is through strife. Although at times it can be difficult, rather than getting into the devil's den by arguing with your child, you can walk away and say, "Get behind me, satan!"

Here's an important point: Arguing is not God's way. If you remain in strife, you are battling on the devil's turf. Guess who wins? – the devil. So what can you do?

Toward the end of 2015, a movie was released called *War Room*. It is a very powerful movie which teaches the grace and love of Jesus Christ and also puts a great emphasis on how to fight with our God-given authority. I would recommend that everyone see it.

In the movie, Miss Clara, using one of the closets in her home, made herself her own war room where she daily met with God.

But thou, when thou prayest, enter into thy closet, and when thou hast shut thy door, pray to the Father which in in secret; and thy Father which seeth in secret shall reward thee openly. (Matt. 6:6)

In the context of Matthew, Chapter 6, it is saying that we should not pray in front of others for show. It's not talking about a literal closet, although there is certainly nothing wrong with using your closet for prayer as depicted in the movie. But let's take this a little further.

Praying to the Father *which is in secret* can also reveal that we fight in prayer using God's Word rather than fighting with our children openly. (2 Corinthians 10:4)

I realized I was getting nowhere with my daughter but at the same time was learning how to take my authority over my real enemy. I stopped fighting with her and started fighting in prayer.

Scripture is clear in telling us that the devil is a crushed and defeated foe:

That through death he [Jesus] might destroy him that had the power of death, that is, the devil. (Hebrews 2:14 - brackets mine)

The Greek meaning of the word *destroy* is

"unemployed; inactivate; to render idle; having no further efficiency; to deprive of force, influence and power; to cause to cease; put an end to; do away with; abolish; annul; to declare invalid (when marriages get annulled, it is as if it never took place); to pass away; to be severed; separated; discharged; loosed from; to terminate all intercourse with one."

Clearly, the devil's work is destroyed! The whole purpose of Jesus coming to earth was so He would destroy the works of the devil:

For this purpose the Son of God was manifested, that He might destroy the works of the devil. (1 John 3:8)

Destroy here means "to dissolve, dismiss, undo, annul, do away with, to deprive of authority, to declare unlawful, break up, demolish, destroy, overthrow."

The devil is defeated; his works are destroyed because of the Cross. If he is already defeated, then why fight him?

When I was praying for Kristin, I wasn't fighting with the enemy as much as I was reminding him of what God's Word said. I reminded him that he is already defeated. He can't steal my peace and my joy, and he certainly has no right to my daughter!

I stood against him when fear and worry tried to grip me. I reminded him that one day *every knee shall bow* (Romans 14:11) and that would include him. I reminded him that I am the head and not the tail, above and not beneath. (Deuteronomy 28:13) I reminded him that no weapon formed against our family shall prosper. (Isaiah 54:17)

According to 2 Corinthians 4:4, I rebuked the god of this world for all his lies and deception he tried to bring on Kristin. I even remember saying, "devil, recess is over!"

In addition, I spoke the Word of God over my situation. I took the sword of the Spirit, which is God's Word (Ephesians 6:17) and spoke life into every situation.

Because Kristin struggled with fear of not being

accepted by her peers, I would claim 2 Timothy 1:7 and declare: "Thank You, Lord, that You have not given Kristin a spirit of fear; but of power, and of love, and of a sound mind." I was literally speaking the complete opposite of what I was seeing, but the Word of God wins every time. Never let your sword down. Always be ready to defend the abundant life Jesus died to give us.

This is how to use the authority God gave you for your children or in any other area about which you may be concerned. As you draw near to God and resist the devil, he has to flee! (James 4:7)

PRAYER:

Thank You, Father, for showing me that _____ is not my real enemy. It is not my child that I need to stand against. I will not allow the enemy to steal my peace and joy as well as my relationship with _____.

Thank You for Your Word which quenches every fiery dart the enemy tries to bring against me and _____.

(Now take your authority and let the devil know that you mean business!)

Chapter 9

Be Careful What You Hear

So then faith cometh by hearing,

and hearing by the word of God.

Romans 10:17

The Bible definition of faith is *the substance of things hoped for, the evidence of things not seen.* (Hebrews 11:1) Simply put, faith is believing that something exists before we can actually see, taste, hear, smell or feel it.

A good example would be Disneyworld. People could have faith that it exists even though they have never seen it with their own eyes. Just because we don't see something doesn't mean it doesn't exist.

From where does faith come? In the book of Romans, Chapter 10, Paul speaks of how we were made righteous by the grace and goodness of God. *Hearing* this message of grace, which is found in His Word, is what causes faith to come to us, as shown in the above scripture.

Why talk about faith when the title of this chapter is "Be Careful What You Hear?"

Let me illustrate with this example: Although only a few people knew about what was going on with our daughter, they had some things to say. Many of those things were not positive. They meant well; they were concerned by voicing their fear and worry about her future, not to mention putting some of the blame for her actions on us. We didn't need to hear these things and had to learn how to fight the fear and doubt that tried to discourage us.

Be careful what you hear. You need to learn what is from God and what is from the devil. The negative things that were said to us were meant to create doubt and unbelief. We knew this much – that doubt is the complete opposite of faith, and it is faith that pleases God:

But without faith it is impossible to please him: for he that cometh to God must believe that he is, and that he is a rewarder of them that diligently seek him. (Hebrews 11:6)

Physical food brings physical strength. Going without it for some time can cause serious problems because we are not being fed what will keep us alive and vibrant.

When we stay in doubt and unbelief because of something we heard, then we are feeding that doubt and it will grow. At the same time doubt grows, we become weaker and weaker, and we actually starve our faith because it is not being fed. Eventually, our faith can no longer do for us what it was meant to do.

Remember that faith comes by hearing and hearing by the Word of God. Unbelief, also, comes by hearing and hearing by the words of the devil. It can work either way.

Hope For Your Children

You are in charge of the words that are spoken to you. You either accept them or reject them. You must protect your heart from words of doubt, fear, and unbelief. But it's your choice.

One way to reject negative words spoken to you would be when you first hear them, recognize them for what they are. If other people are saying, "She is just too young to have a baby. She is going to have a hard life," this is not according to God's Word. You, in turn, can reply with scripture: "My Jesus came to give my daughter abundant life and she has it." (John 10:10) "My God is, and always will be faithful to my daughter." (2 Timothy 2:13) "He never leaves her nor forsakes her." (Hebrews 13:5) Speaking verses like this out loud will render the statements of fear, doubt, and unbelief, useless.

I remember when I was dealing with weird physical symptoms which lasted for weeks. I didn't tell anyone, except my husband. I had a couple of wonderful Christian lady friends with whom I could have shared it. They would have spoken positive things and given words of life to me, but I didn't want

Be Careful What You Hear

to hear *myself* speaking out loud the symptoms I was experiencing. Why? I was protecting my own heart. I knew that if I heard those symptoms, even if it was coming out of my own mouth, it could have caused fear and unbelief. Weeks later, my friends discovered for the first time what I was experiencing through a testimony I gave of my miraculous healing!

There will be negative people in your life who will speak negative things. Don't give those words a second thought. In the Garden of Eden, God told Adam that he could eat of any tree except for the Tree of the Knowledge of Good and Evil. In Genesis, Chapter 3, the devil tempted Eve to eat of the tree. After Eve explained that they were not permitted to eat of it or they would die, look what the serpent said:

And the serpent said unto the woman, Ye shall not surely die: For God doth know that in the day ye eat thereof, then your eyes shall be opened, and ye shall be as gods, knowing good and evil. (vv. 4-5)

Now let's look at Eve's response:

And when the woman saw that the tree was good for food, and that it was pleasant to the eyes, and a tree to be desired to make one wise, she took of the fruit thereof, and did eat, and gave also unto her husband with her; and he did eat. (v. 6)

And when the woman saw... is when Eve blew it. The serpent was able to tempt her to consider another alternative other than God's will. Eve was content at first that they were not permitted to eat of the tree, but the devil perverted the truth and continued to lie to her, until she took the bait. She gave those lies a second thought the moment she turned and looked at the tree.

Eating the fruit cost them everything; sin entered the world and they lost their authority and dominion over the earth. The devil was now the god of this world. Thank God for Jesus, that through faith and belief in Him, dominion and authority has been given back to us through the cross. It's just up to us to receive it.

Fill your mind with the Word of God. Don't wait

until something happens to find your Bible and study it – there may not be time for that. Be transformed by the renewing of your mind and be ready to reject anything negative that comes to your ears and replace it with words of life.

And be not conformed to this world: but be ye transformed by the renewing of your mind, that ye may prove what is that good, and acceptable, and perfect, will of God. (Romans 12:2)

PRAYER:
Thank You, Lord, that You have given me something I can do when people speak negative things about _____ to me.

I make a commitment today to reject whatever I hear that is against Your Word regarding my child and replace it with Your words of life. I choose to renew my mind so that I will be ready to counter anything I hear that opposes Your Word.

Thank You, Lord. In Jesus Name, Amen.

Chapter 10

Forgive

And when ye stand praying, forgive, if ye have ought against any: that your Father also which is in heaven may forgive you your trespasses.

Mark 11:25

Mark 11:23 and 24 teaches us to speak to the mountains, or problems, in our lives and to know that whatever we pray, if we believe we receive what we are asking for, then we shall have it:

For verily I say unto you, That whosoever shall say unto this mountain, Be thou removed, and be thou cast into the sea; and shall not doubt in his heart, but shall believe that those things which he saith shall come to pass; he shall have whatsoever he saith. Therefore I say unto you, What things soever ye desire, when ye pray, believe that ye receive them, and ye shall have them.

This is a clear picture of the authority of the believer we discussed in Chapter 8.

Verse 25 instructs us that as we pray this way, we must forgive those we have ought against:

And when ye stand praying, forgive, if ye have ought against any: that your Father also which is in heaven may forgive you your trespasses.

God places forgiveness in the realm of prayer. This clearly means that unforgiveness can be a big hindrance to answered prayer.

If you harbor the hurt you may feel from your children doing as they please, you need to deal with it immediately. Sometimes, that hurt will turn into bitterness, which can turn into anger.

When you become bitter and angry, you are in unforgiveness. It will not matter how correct your speech life is, or how much authority you take over

Forgive

the situation. If you won't forgive, your prayers will be blocked.

Why is forgiveness so important to God? Because He sent His Son, Jesus, to suffer great punishment and death so that we could be forgiven. It cost the Father a great deal – His Son – to wipe our slate clean before Him. The heart of the Father is forgiveness, and He has extended that forgiveness toward us because He loves us. Shouldn't we forgive others as He has forgiven us?

...Forbearing one another, and forgiving one another, if any man have a quarrel against any: even as Christ forgave you, so also do ye. (Colossians 3:13)

I had forgiveness issues during the trials with Kristin. She wasn't the only one I had to forgive, although it seemed that I could easily forgive her because she was my daughter. I think parents are so ready to forgive their own children. It was a bit harder to forgive the friends that tempted her, as well as her boyfriend/husband. Kristin's husband's actions made it very hard for me to forgive him.

I knew very clearly what the Bible had to say about forgiveness. I knew I had to forgive, but I didn't know how. I *wanted* to forgive because I knew that it was what God wanted.

God wants us to forgive because it frees us from all the junk we hold inside which can lead to stress, depression, and physical sickness. We are hurting ourselves more than the people we refuse to forgive.

Forgiveness also releases others from any debt that you think they owe you. By forgiving, you are letting them go. Once you do this, God is now free to work in their life. As long as you are holding them to a debt, He cannot get to them. Jesus wiped out our debt; we need to wipe out the debt we think others owe us.

We may feel that some people do not deserve our forgiveness because of what they have done to us. You're probably right; they may not deserve it. But do we deserve God's forgiveness for what we have done? Not at all! Thank God for His grace in that He treats us as if we have never sinned. We should show that same grace to others.

When you forgive, you are pardoning someone from penalty. Jesus did that for us by dying on the cross. You are forever freed from the guilt and penalty of sin.

How do we know if we need to forgive? In addition to just pure anger, there are underlying emotions that reveal there is unforgiveness, such as fear and sadness. When you think of a particular person and you feel anger, fear, or sadness, you will usually find unforgiveness at the root of those emotions.

What many Christians do not understand is that forgiveness starts first with a desire, then with a decision. Some do not have any desire to forgive. I know a few people like this, but it will eventually be to their detriment. If you do not desire to forgive, then ask God to give you that desire, and He will create it within you.

Once the desire is there, then a decision must be

made to actually forgive. This decision is not based on feelings; it is based on faith. Let's look at Luke 17:4-5:

And if he trespass against thee seven times in a day, and seven times in a day turn again to thee, saying, I repent; thou shalt forgive him. And the apostles said unto the Lord, Increase our faith.

Notice the apostles realized that they needed faith to forgive; they could not forgive without it. Forgiveness is not based on how we feel. Our feelings are not the issue – faith is. So deciding to forgive is simply an act of faith.

As I said earlier, I wanted to forgive Kristin's husband and made the decision to do so. The first thing I did was to speak out loud, "I forgive him." As often as I thought about him, I said it. Every thought of him brought anger, fear and sadness, but I combatted those feelings with the Word of God.

After the divorce, Kristin received full custody of my grandson, Matthew. We still had contact with Kristin's ex-husband and some of his family because they wanted to see Matthew. Our way of showing love to them was to allow them to visit him. We had them come to our home for certain holidays, or whenever they called to see him. This, after a while, faded away. But at least we did the right thing during that time. This was just another way of showing our decision to forgive. We really never felt right being around them, but again, forgiveness is not a feeling; it's a decision.

I also attended a weekly prayer meeting and each week we lifted him up in prayer, praying for his salvation, rebuking the god of this world that had him deceived (2 Cor. 4:4), and asking that someone would come into his life to minister the love and grace of Jesus Christ. (Luke 10:2) As I prayed this each week, my heart began to soften toward him. Today, if he showed up at our home, we would welcome him, as we did years ago.

But there is even a deeper forgiveness that we can experience. When we mediate and get revelation on how much God really loves us, we begin to experience that love and it comes alive in us. If we desire and decide to forgive, it is this God kind of love that pours out from us to others. When that happens, we will look at them totally different than we did before; all that they may have done to hurt us is faded in the background and means absolutely nothing to us any longer. The love of God permeates every thought of them.

A good way to begin to understand the depth of God's love for you is to read out loud and meditate on 1st Corinthians, Chapter 13. Pastor Bobby Ray of the Assembly of Faith Church in Dallas, North Carolina, set up a great way to mediate on the truth of this passage. He calls it *The Gospills*. Read the passage as is, then read it again replacing the word "love" with "God." Then read it again replacing the word "love" with "I." Ask God to reveal His love for you so that you can love and forgive others as He loves and has forgiven you. There's nothing like it!

Love endures long and is patient and kind; love never is envious nor boils over with jealousy, is not boastful or vainglorious, does not display itself haughtily. It is not conceited (arrogant and inflated with pride); it is not rude (unmannerly) and does not act unbecomingly. Love (God's love in us) does not insist on its own rights or its own way, for it is not self-seeking; it is not touchy or fretful or resentful; it takes no account of the evil done to it [it pays no attention to a suffered wrong]. It does not rejoice at injustice and unrighteousness, but rejoices when right and truth prevail. Love bears up under anything and everything that comes, is ever ready to believe the best of every person, its hopes are fadeless under all circumstances, and it endures everything [without weakening]. Love never fails [never fades out or becomes obsolete or comes to an end]. 1st Cor. 13:1-8 (Amplified Translation, Classic Edition)

PRAYER:

I realize now that forgiveness is a choice and not a feeling. Thank You, Lord, for revealing this to me.

Thank you that I can do all things because you strengthen me. (Philippians 4:13) I truly desire to forgive and by faith I make the decision to forgive_____.

In Jesus Name, Amen.

Chapter 11

Giving

Give, and it shall be given unto you;
good measure, pressed down, and shaken together,
and running over, shall men give into your bosom.
For with the same measure that ye mete withal it shall
be measured to you again.

Luke 6:38

There are many ways to give. The Scriptures leading up to Luke 6:38 show some of those ways. They all fall under the one and only law for new-covenant believers – the law of love.

Let's look at some ways the Bible teaches us to give: Giving out good to those who hate you (Luke 6:27); Give blessings to those who curse you (v. 28);

Take time to pray for those who spitefully use you (v. 28); Give even more material possessions to those who take from you and do not ask for them back (vv. 29 & 30); Treat others the way you want to be treated (v. 31); Give out love, do good, and lend, hoping for nothing in return (v. 35); Give mercy (v. 36); Refrain from judging and condemning and give out forgiveness. (v. 37)

I love the end of Luke 6:38 – *...For with the same measure that ye mete withal it shall be measured to you again.* What a great promise! If we bless, give, love, forgive and have mercy toward others, those same blessings will come back to us when we need it.

Another way the Bible teaches us to give is with our money, such as lending without expecting a return. (Luke 6:35)

But what does giving have to do with resolving some of the issues with our children? Everything! When we give, we set ourselves up for miracles to be manifested in our lives. When we give, it will be given back to us good measure, pressed down,

Giving

shaken together and running over. But it doesn't necessarily have to come back in money.

There are numerous stories in the Bible about people who were givers. When they had a need, other than money, their need was met. I will focus on one of the stories that I believe will relate to you and your children.

Second Kings, 4:8-37 is the story of the prophet Elisha who was passing through the town of Shunem and was invited to eat at the home of a woman and her husband. In fact, every time the prophet came through their town, the woman fed him.

The Bible says that she compelled him to eat at her home. She recognized him as a prophet of God and decided to make a bedroom for him to use, whenever he passed by.

This woman was a giver. Not only did it cost her money to feed Elisha, but it cost money to build a room for him. Elisha traveled with his servant, Gehazi, and I believe that she fed and housed his servant, as well. This is just my opinion.

Hope For Your Children

Elisha did not take her kindness and giving for granted. He wanted to do something for her. Knowing that she never bore a child and her husband was old, Elisha prophesied that she would have a son. She was reluctant to believe it. She longed for a child and was in shock when she heard this. She told the prophet not to lie to her; not long after that, she conceived.

As the child grew older, he worked in the fields with his father. One day, while working, his head began to hurt. One of the servants carried the boy to his mother, and he died as she held him on her lap. She immediately put him on Elisha's bed, shut the door to his room and left to find the prophet.

I believe that the relationship between the Shunemite woman and Elisha lasted for years and that she consistently gave to him. Now she needed him for a miracle - and she got it. She brought Elisha back to the house to pray over her son, and he was raised back to life!

Is your son or daughter spiritually dead? Have they run away from God? They can be brought back

Giving

to life through your giving. Let me share what we did with Kristin and still do today.

My husband and I are givers. We make sure we plant our giving into good ground, such as our local church or to outside ministries that are teaching the whole counsel of God. Nothing leaves our hand without giving it an assignment.

We both lay hands on our offering and purpose it to whatever we may be needing at the time. We definitely believe we will receive 100 fold return on all our giving, but there are many times we believe for other things, as well.

Once Kristin married her boyfriend, things got even worse. Due to several different felonies, he was continually in and out of jail. They sold their home, and Kristin used all her money to bail him out each time. There were times he would leave their house to go to the store and not return for days.

One night Kristin awoke at 3 am and her husband was no where to be found. She and the baby went outside to look for him and got locked out of the house. (I found that out later on, from a friend.) He never worked and totally neglected my daughter and grandson. When their lights and electricity were about to be turned off, it was my daughter who had to go out and get a job. It was a mess.

Shortly after their divorce, I remember one evening when I talked with him on the phone because he was threatening our family. I was firm; he began mocking me, so I hung up the phone. I went to a church service that night; the Lord told me to write a check out for $500.00 and mail it to a certain ministry with the purpose of getting him out of our lives. As soon as I returned home, I did just that.

One week later my daughter informed me that he was arrested in another state and would be there for at least five years. Praise God! It has been many years since that time. Because of our giving, this man never even attempts to reach us.

This worked super fast for us because we had already been givers for years. It may take some time before you see the fruit of giving. Mark 4:28 says,

Giving

For the earth bringeth forth fruit of herself; first the blade, then the ear, after that the full corn in the ear. A farmer does not see his harvest all at once; it takes time to grow. Be patient; give and believe God for your harvest.

I am not saying that we can buy God's goodness. What I am saying is that I sowed a seed because I had a need, and the need was met.

This is living by faith. It's the way God designed it, and we can experience His blessings everyday.

Giving works, but it is in combination with the other things we learned in this book. You cannot give for your children while you are speaking words of doubt and unbelief, or by allowing strife within your family, or by not praying correctly, or by not taking your authority. It all works together, but giving is a vital part of seeing your desires manifested.

All these principles in God's Word that we are encouraged to live by are for us, so that we can experience the abundant life Jesus died to give us. We can be a witness to the world of just how faithful and good God is.

I encourage you to give; you can't afford not to!

PRAYER:
Thank You, Lord, for showing me the importance of giving. I understand I am not buying a miracle, but I also believe that my seed will meet my need of seeing my child restored.

Thank You that_____ will be raised to life again! Thank You that my child will honor and serve You all the days of his/her life. Thank You for Your faithfulness to our family.

In Jesus Name, Amen.

Chapter 12

Don't Give Up!

Blessed is the man that endureth temptation: for when he is tried, he shall receive the crown of life, which the Lord hath promised to them that love him.

James 1:12

There were times I thought I would never see the day when my daughter would be settled and happy again. The struggles that arose as a result of her decisions seemed to continue for years, but in reality, and in the scheme of things, it was for a short time.

I'm sure you have heard the phrase, "This too shall pass." I believe this is true in any trial we may be facing.

There is another similar phrase that is used

hundreds of times in Scripture: "And it came to pass..." Although this really means "it happened," it's been humorously stated, "and it (your trial) doesn't come to stay - it comes to pass."

Trials do not have to last a lifetime, but I believe the duration and outcome of any trial depends mostly on us.

In a previous chapter I mentioned that some years ago I experienced quite serious physical symptoms. They lasted for three weeks, but it felt like three years. I believe these symptons could have lasted three full years or longer if I did not fight the good fight of faith by standing on the Word and protecting what was rightfully mine, such as health, peace, joy, and victory. We not only can shorten the length of our trials, but we also can have a testimony of victory at the end of it.

I've seen many Christian parents give up. They don't give up on their children, but because they become weary they give up on their anger over sin, the devil, and any unrighteousness that seems to

Don't Give Up!

have overtaken their children. You may feel tired and drained; but, parents, I encourage you to not give up!

Let's look at what I believe to be one of the most misunderstood scriptures in the Bible:

Be ye angry, and sin not: let not the sun go down upon your wrath: Neither give place to the devil. (Ephesians 4:26-27)

Most Christians believe this means that we are never to go to bed angry at anyone; we have to make sure we settle our differences before we turn in for the night.

It is true that we shouldn't be angry with others, day or night, but this scripture is not talking about being angry with people; it's talking about an anger against sin and the devil. If we are angry at others, then it is sin. However, there is an anger that is not sin; it's called a righteous anger.

To *not* be angry at the devil is wrong. This verse is instructing us to never give up on being angry at evil. We must be relentless. Even when we sleep at night, we should never stop having this righteous anger. What this verse is really saying is not to let your anger go to sleep! If your anger weakens, then you are giving place to the devil. Wow!

There is no room for passivity in the life of a Christian. If we want victory in our lives, then we must be aggressive. Whether we like it or not, we are in a continual spiritual battle; lazy people do not win battles. It's just a matter of what you want, how much you really want it, and how far you will go to get it.

In 1 Samuel, Chapter 17, young David meets the giant, Goliath, head-on. The giant dared David to come closer to him. But this did not move David at all. He stood strong and said:

...Thou comest to me with a sword, and with a spear, and with a shield: but I come to thee in the name of the Lord of hosts, the God of the armies of Israel, whom thou hast defied. This day will the Lord deliver thee into mine hand; and I will smite thee, and take thine head from thee; and I will give

Don't Give Up!

the carcasses of the host of the Philistines this day unto the fowls of the air, and to the wild beasts of the earth; that all the earth may know that there is a God in Israel. And all this assembly shall know that the Lord saveth not with sword and spear: for the battle is the Lord's, and he will give you into our hands. (vv. 45-47)

This is an authority prayer! The next verse tells us that rather than David running *from* his enemy, he ran *toward* him:

And it came to pass, when the Philistine arose, and came, and drew nigh to meet David, that David hastened, and ran toward the army to meet the Philistine. (v. 48)

Rather than fearing our enemy, we need to stand up to him. We should be aggressive for our children in the midst of their struggle; we must stand for them. We must speak protection, wisdom, and favor over them. We must stand on every promise in the Word of God until we see it manifested. And we must always be on guard because the enemy roams around like a roaring lion seeking whom he may devour. If you give him permission, then he will devour you and your child. (1 Peter 5:8)

It may look like this is working for *you*, the parent, but not for your child. You may have experienced victory in your mind with peace, joy, and confidence, but nothing seems to change with your child. Not to worry!

Your staying in peace is vital to you as a parent for a couple of reasons. First, it is only when we are in peace that we can actually hear from God. Second, your peace and joy will bring great confidence while praying for your children. According to Mark 11:24, when you believe what you pray, you shall have it.

Let's again look at the Scripture found at the very beginning of this chapter:

Blessed is the man that endureth temptation: for when he is tried, he shall receive the crown of life, which the Lord hath promised to them that love him. (James 1:12)

Don't Give Up!

The word *endureth* does not mean to put up with; the original Greek meaning is "to persevere." The original meaning of the word *temptation* means "trials." We are blessed when we persevere through trials. We are also promised the crown of life when we don't give up.

If you want things to change in your family, you can't afford to give up; you may find yourself drained and even crying at times. It's okay if you shed those tears; just don't stay there! Get up; take your sword; continue to be angry, and stand for what is rightfully yours!

PRAYER:
Father, I thank You that no trial lasts forever. I declare now that I will never give up on my anger toward sin and the devil. Forgive me for being passive at times.

I choose to fight the good fight of faith by defending everything that You accomplished for me and my family at the cross 2000 years ago.

Thank You for helping me to persevere through this

difficulty with_____.

In Jesus Name, Amen.

Chapter 13

Kristin's Story

You have heard my side of the story, but I thought it would be helpful to hear from my daughter, also. You will be blessed.

Kristin:

I was brought up in a Christian home. I gave my life to Jesus during my elementary school years at a children's program in our church.

As I entered middle school age, the small town I lived in was becoming boring to me. I remember looking at my yearbook cover which showed a beautiful underwater scene. I loved it and started thinking that there had to be more to this world than just this town.

I was curious and had a strong sense of adventure which was good and bad at the same time. I knew there wasn't anything wrong with having these desires, but it made me feel super tied down. I always felt that I was missing something.

While desiring this sense of adventure, my peers at middle school posed a problem. My parents would not allow me to do some of the activities other kids at school were doing. They believed that what I watched and what I heard would affect me greatly, so they would not allow me to listen to certain music or watch certain movies.

I felt held back which caused great embarrassment with my classmates. I was more on the quiet side to begin with, but others looking down on me made me even more introverted. Being called a "goody-goody" hurt badly. I was not accepted at school, so I would just hang out with the kids in my neighborhood. I realize now that this was a form of persecution for living the life of a Christian, both for me and my family.

Kristin's Story

The funny thing is that I never tried to be like my peers; I never tried to fit in. In fact, after a while, I developed a distaste for them. In my opinion, they were snobs and they turned me off.

Although my parents set boundaries for me, I was never angry with them for doing so. Deep inside I knew they were doing the right thing, and that's mainly because they loved me and taught me the Word of God at an early age.

Not connecting with those at school led me to the real "cool" people (who weren't really cool), who seemed to accept me. They did not attend my school. They accepted me for who I was and that felt good.

But they were a bad influence on me. I began drinking, breaking curfews, skipping classes and dropped out of school in 11th grade, even though I had a 4.0 grade point average.

I knew without a doubt that I was rebelling against my parents and God. But it did not stop me. I believed the lie of the enemy, constantly telling me that there was more to life than what I was experiencing. I wanted it all.

I eventually became angry with the "cool" people because they would try to get me to do things that I knew would hurt my parents. It was weird because I obviously was hurting them all along, yet that didn't seem to bother me. But I drew a line in the sand. I really do not believe that most children want to intentionally hurt their parents. I am totally convinced it was because of the position my parents took in prayer that I quit hanging out with that group.

However, when I turned seventeen, I met another group of friends. Being "bad" was "cool" back then and probably still is today. The first night I was with this new group, they were doing drugs; I knew they were bad news. I really didn't want to try drugs, but it was new and exciting. I was still looking for adventure. Someone offered me a pill to make me feel better – they told me I would love it. So I thought to myself, "What can one pill do?" It felt great. The next day I wanted it again. I was part of something and it felt good. Little did I know that being bad was not cool at all, but stupid.

Kristin's Story

I did not want to be home; I broke every rule in the house. I wanted freedom. The funny thing is that my parents were very good to me and my siblings. They loved us and treated us awesomely; we never lacked anything. They always taught us to do the right thing and protected us from what they believed could harm us.

During that time I met a charming playboy type guy with whom I became infatuated. I crossed the line with him and felt guilty the entire time.

As a result of my actions, my parents told me to leave our house. I did not know at the time that God had told them to put me out. I lived with my boyfriend in an airport hanger for three months, which I thought was fun. I saw my parents twice in those three months, and it was awkward for both of us. I was confused why they didn't welcome me. I was so deceived by the devil at this point that I didn't even think I was in rebellion. I was totally "had" by the enemy. The devil had continual "recess" in my mind and filled it with lies, lies, lies, but I took it as truth.

Hope For Your Children

I became pregnant because I wanted to. My girlfriends valued me because they were all pregnant, too. I never gave a thought to my future. I was just fulfilling every lust I had.

But a funny thing happened when I found out I was pregnant. From that moment on, I wanted to make everything right. I wanted to go back to living the way my parents taught me. I felt I accomplished what I had wanted and was content about it.

I wrote my parents a sincere letter of apology, along with the news that they would be grandparents. I never once thought how all this was affecting them because I didn't see anything wrong with it at the time. The enemy had me so confused and duped.

I married my boyfriend and it was a disaster. He blamed me for everything and neglected our baby and me. He would tell me he was going to the store and be gone for three days. I felt completely rejected and unloved. He went to jail many times for various felonies, and I used up all of our money to bail him out. This is important – Although my parents were

Kristin's Story

suffering inside, they showed me love and grace through this entire ordeal. They treated me just like Jesus would. I'll never forget that.

I finally decided I couldn't do it any longer. After three years, we were divorced and I got full custody of my son. Here's the good news:

After the divorce, I was faced with many emotional issues. It was hard at times, but I had the full support of my parents. I lived in a small house on their property, and they helped me, tremendously.

I poured myself into what I knew to be the answer all along – God's Word. I meditated on scriptures and watched some of the sermons that were on TV which helped me greatly. I attended a Bible study and had fellowship with other believers. On a regular basis, I also met with a Christian counselor, who was a huge help.

Today, I am a completely different person. I am still curious and adventurous, but in a positive way. The grace and goodness of God freed me from all bondages and rejection issues, and I love Him with all my heart. The Lord sent me a wonderful man who is now my husband. He is fully committed to loving and raising my son, who is now fifteen years old and an awesome young man full of love and compassion for others.

I am an interior designer and a life coach. My husband and I own a small business. We are blessed beyond measure!

Parents, I urge you to follow the principles my mom outlined in this book. Both my parents stood by me, through it all. If they hadn't, I would not be writing this chapter today.

Some would say that it was probably good that I went through all those things because now I am able to help others with the same issues. No, it wasn't good. I may have learned some things, but my behavior was never good; God never intended for me to rebel. It was my own choice. The part that God played was to extend both His grace and mercy to me, then and now.

When I was about nine years old, I remember

Kristin's Story

in the middle of the night standing at my mother's bed, crying. She asked me what was wrong and I admitted that I did not return a library book that was due that day. I felt guilty and said to her, "I don't know why I did this; I really don't want to be this way." She comforted me and assured me that I did the right thing by admitting it, rather than hiding it, and was glad that I was truly sorry.

I am not making excuses; I know I did wrong things. But I was so confused. Deep inside of me, I always knew God was there. I was a Christian, yet I chose to make wrong decisions.

I really believe even when I had a care-less attitude, deep down in my heart I did not want to act the way I did. Your children probably feel the same way, especially if they were brought up in a Christian home learning Christian values.

Do not despair; what God did for me, He will do for you and your child. He is no respecter of persons. (Romans 2:11) I am so very grateful to my parents for obeying what God told them to do and say. It saved my life. I urge you, as my mom said in the last chapter, do not give up on God and His love for you and your child. Do not give up on your authority over evil. It may look like things will never change, and that's what the devil wants you to believe. Things *will* change; just keep standing and believing.

We win! To God be the glory!

Final Thoughts

Although this book is focused on how to deal with trials regarding our children, the truths that I outlined can apply to every area of your life.

You may be in need of physical healing or financial freedom; you may have just lost your job and can't seem to find another; you may have a child that is sick, or you may have just lost a loved one. Whatever the problem, the solution lies within these pages.

As I was sitting in my backyard, gazing across the lake, I noticed all the trees on the other side were the same height. Then I looked above the trees and God spoke to me, "Angie, I want you to always live above the trees."

He then asked me what I noticed below the trees. I answered, "...houses, pools, boats, people, and many other things." God pointed out to me that if I live below the trees, depending on what I see, taste, hear, smell, and feel, then I will become distracted and confused.

But if I live in the greater reality, which is the presence of God, Himself, I will experience all His promises in my life.

If I am faced with a trial, and I choose to be distracted by thinking and operating in the natural realm, then I'll get very little, if any, results.

But, if I focus on the greater reality and esteem God's Word above all difficulty, then I will experience abundant life in every way.

Parents, stay above the trees! Don't look down – look up and you will find all that you could ever want or need. (Colossians 3:2)

God is our cheerleader. He is always encouraging us as He leads and guides us to the path of victory.

Final Thoughts

One of my favorite scriptures is Zephaniah 3:17:

The Lord thy God in the midst of thee is mighty; he will save, he will rejoice over thee with joy; he will rest in his love, he will joy over thee with singing.

The original meaning of the word *joy* is "to spin around." God is ecstatic over us! He is the strength of our life; He defends and delivers us. He can rest in His love for us simply because there is no love that is greater. He sings, spins, and dances over us and our children with joy.

Let's enjoy His love!

Prayer for Your Children

Father, thank You for Your grace. Thank You that You provided everything I will ever need at the cross. Thank You for taking care of my child, _____.

I take my authority in the Name of Jesus and rebuke you, satan. You get out of _____'s thought life; take your lies and your schemes with you! Let me remind you that you are a crushed and defeated foe, and I laugh at all your powerless attempts to destroy my child. You may try to come against me and _____ with your tricks and deception, but I come against you in the name of the Lord Jesus

Hope For Your Children

Christ, whose power no foe can withstand!

I place a hedge of protection around my child. Thank You, Father, that Your angels are always watching over _____. Thank You that my child is protected from all evil, harm, accidents, and sickness.

Father, thank You that You are sending someone into my child's life to minister Your message of Love and Grace. I thank You, Holy Spirit, that You are opening up the gates of_____'s heart to You. Thank You for convicting my child of sin while revealing Your mercy to_____. And thank You that when _____ hears Your Word, faith will rise and revelation will lead _____ to a personal relationship with You.

In Jesus Name, Amen.

Prayer For Your Children

Words Have Creative Power!
Confess daily for you and your children

- I have the mind of Christ. (1 Cor. 2:16)
- I am a new creature in Christ. (2 Cor. 5:17)
- I am the righteousness of God in Christ Jesus. (2 Cor. 5:21)
- I am victorious. (1 Cor. 15:57)
- I walk by faith and not by sight. (2 Cor. 5:7)
- I am overtaken with blessings. (Deut. 28:2)
- My prayers availeth much. (James 5:16)
- I am more than a conqueror. (Romans 8:37)
- I will fear no evil, for You are with me. (Psalm 23:4)
- No weapon formed against me will prosper. (Isaiah 54:17)
- No evil will befall me. (Psalm 91:10)
- You have given your angels charge over me. (Psalm 91:11)
- The devil flees from me because I resist him. (James 4:7)
- My children are taught of the Lord. (Isaiah 54:13)
- Great is the peace of my children. (Isaiah 54:13)
- The Lord is the strength of my life. (Psalm 27:1)
- I refuse to give place to the devil. (Eph. 4:27)

Hope For Your Children

- I let the peace of God rule in my heart. (Col. 3:15)
- I am complete in Him. (Col. 2:10)
- The joy of the Lord is my strength. (Nehemiah 8:10)
- He will perfect that which concerns me. (Psalm 138:8)

Prayer for You

Prayer to Receive Jesus as Your Lord and Savior

This is where your new life begins. Once you receive His gift of salvation, you become brand new with the nature of God residing on the inside of you!

To receive Jesus as your Lord and Savior and to become born again, simply pray the following prayer aloud:

Jesus, I am sorry for my sins. I believe You died for my sins and that God raised You from the dead. I receive Your forgiveness, and I make You the Savior and Lord of my life. Thank You for saving me.

Congratulations! You are now a brand-new creation. Your Spirit man is forever changed:

Therefore if any man be in Christ, he is a new creature: old things are passed away; behold, all things are become new. (2 Cor. 5:17)

Prayer to Receive the Baptism of the Holy Spirit

God's desire is to empower you to live your new life. Jesus, Himself, was baptized in the Holy Spirit before He ever began His public ministry. If Jesus needed it, then we need it, as well. (Matt. 3:13-17) This is a separate experience from being born-again. (Acts 8:14-17) Salvation saves; Baptism in the Holy Spirit empowers.

The gift of tongues is immediately available to you once you are baptized in the Holy Spirit. (Acts 10:44-46) Speaking in tongues is the Holy Spirit praying God's will through you. Your part is to allow it.

Purpose of Speaking in Tongues:

1) It promotes spiritual growth - 1 Cor. 14: 2 & 4 (edifies you)

2) It keeps you aware of, and enjoying God's Love -

Jude 1:20-21

3) It produces rest and spiritual refreshment - Isaiah 28:11-12

4) It is giving thanks well - 1 Cor. 14:17

5) It releases revelation knowledge - 1 Cor. 14:18 - Paul says: *I thank my God, I speak in tongues more than ye all.* Connect this with the fact that Paul wrote two-thirds of the New Testament. Paul spent 3 years with God alone in the desert where he received wisdom and revelation knowledge by praying in tongues.

Speaking in tongues is vital in the life of a Christian. You must desire it, ask for it, believe and receive it.

To receive the baptism in the Holy Spirit with the evidence of speaking in tongues, pray the following prayer aloud:

Lord, I want to be empowered to live this new life. I know this is a gift from You, and I need it to live the abundant life You've promised me. Please fill me now with Your Holy Spirit with the evidence

Prayer For You

of speaking in tongues. Thank You for baptizing me. By faith, I fully expect to speak in other tongues as You give me the utterance. (Acts 2:4)

In Jesus Name, Amen.

Now begin thanking and praising God for baptizing you, and begin speaking the syllables He gives you. This is the language the Holy Spirit has given to you. To speak this language aloud is an act of your will by faith. God will never force you to speak—it will always be your decision.

Enjoy your new personal spiritual language as often as you like, and as you do, you will build yourself up in your faith: *But ye, beloved, building up yourselves on your most holy faith, praying in the Holy Ghost.* (Jude 1:20)

If you'd like additional information regarding salvation or the baptism of the Holy Spirit, please see the resources at the end of this book.

Suggested Readings

There are many nuggets of truth that need to be mined out of God's Word in the same way the woman searched diligently until she found her lost coin. (Luke 15:8-10) I recommend the following books for an in-depth teaching on **WHO** we are in Christ, **WHAT** we have in Christ, and **HOW** to use what we have been given:

Spirit, Soul & Body by Andrew Wommack: The **WHO**; this book provides foundational teaching, describing what actually happens when we are born again. It explains how we are made of three parts, one of which is our Spirit man that becomes brand new when we make Jesus our Lord and Savior.

You've Already Got It! (So Quit Trying to Get It) by Andrew Wommack: The **WHAT**; whatever it is we need, we already have! Through this book, you'll learn how everything we could ever need was provided by Jesus at the cross. Knowing what we actually have inside our born-again spirit motivates us to change the negative circumstances in our lives.

The Believer's Authority: What You Didn't Learn in Church by Andrew Wommack: The **HOW**; this book will teach you how to recognize satan's tactics and how to fight against them in order to win every battle in your life.

The New You and The Holy Spirit by Andrew Wommack: Learn exactly what transpires when you make the decision to follow the Lord and become born again, as well as the benefits you receive through the baptism in the Holy Spirit.

You can order these books and more at: www.awmi.net.

Suggested Readings

God's Best Is for You, Too! by Al and Angie Buhrke: Al and Angie share their personal stories of trials and triumphs. This book is an encouragement to those facing trials in their lives by showing how staying single-minded on the Word of God produces positive results.

Hidden Treasures Revealed by Angie Buhrke: Angie shares the treasures in God's Word that will help anyone live a victorious life. This book shows God's plan for His children to live above their circumstances, not beneath them. Understanding the truths within this book will help you do just that!

You can order these books by email:
victorylife.aa@gmail.com

Contact Information:

Angie Buhrke

victorylifeministries.org

E-Mail: victorylife.aa@gmail.com